Stop Smoking

Numerous Cessation Strategies For Smoking That
Facilitate Immediate And Permanent Smoking Cessation

*(Tobacco Cessation Is The Key To A Happier, Healthier Life
And Independence)*

Dr. Charles Turcotte

TABLE OF CONTENT

The Benefits Of Quitting Smoking 1

The Significance Of Kicking The Habit At A Young Age 10

Advice On Determining When To Stop Working And Making Arrangements For The Change ... 14

Methods For Breaking The Habit 16

Alcohol Is Smoking's Ugly Sibling. 27

Choosing A Date To Quit 36

Go Forward And Present A Goal. 40

Slow Disengagement 45

The Prevalence Of The Stigma Is Astounding . 65

Maintaining Success Over The Long Term While Trying To Avoid Failure 70

The Phenomenon Of Putting On Weight After Giving Up Smoking 76

The Repercussions Of Smoking, Both Physiologically And Mentally.................................80

The Numerous Advantages Of Giving Up Smoking...88

How To Remain Smoke-Free Once You Have Quit..95

Finding It Difficult To Kick The Habit While You're Pregnant?...105

The Importance Of The Role Of Social Support 111

Begin Making Your Plans Right Away!.............118

Facts Regarding People Who Smoke................130

The Benefits Of Quitting Smoking

Putting an end to your smoking habit can have a positive impact on your overall health and well-being. The following is a list of some of the most important advantages of giving up smoking:

Quitting smoking will greatly reduce your risk of acquiring lung cancer as well as other types of cancer, such as bladder, cervical, esophageal, kidney, liver, pancreatic, and stomach cancers. Quitting smoking will also reduce your risk of heart disease.

Better lung function is one benefit of quitting smoking, along with a reduction in the symptoms of chronic obstructive pulmonary disease (COPD) and other respiratory disorders.

Quitting smoking can help improve your cardiovascular health in a number of ways, including lowering your risk of heart disease and stroke, lowering your blood pressure, and improving your circulation.

Quitting smoking can boost fertility in both men and women, making it simpler to conceive and increase the likelihood of a successful pregnancy.

Quitting smoking can increase your sense of smell and taste, allowing you to take fuller pleasure in the flavors of the foods and beverages you consume.

Quitting smoking can help improve the appearance of your teeth and give you fresher breath. Smoking can cause teeth to turn yellow and give people terrible breath, but quitting smoking can help improve the appearance of your teeth and give you fresher breath.

Quitting smoking is associated with a reduction in the appearance of wrinkles and other symptoms of aging, as well as an improvement in the skin's overall health and appearance.

Quitting smoking can help you save a large amount of money over time, especially considering how pricey cigarettes are and how quickly their cost mounts up over time.

stopping smoking can help your sense of smell and taste recover and become more sensitive. Smoking can dull your sense of smell and taste, but stopping can help recover and restore these senses.

Quitting smoking is associated with a reduction in the severity of symptoms associated with anxiety and depression, as well as an improvement in overall mental health and well-being.

Quitting smoking can enhance lung capacity as well as stamina, making it simpler to exercise and ultimately leading to improvements in athletic performance.

Quitting smoking not only has positive effects on your personal health, but it also lowers the danger of secondhand smoke exposure for people who are in your immediate environment.

Quitting smoking demands discipline and self-control, which, in addition to helping boost confidence and self-esteem, can result in an improved sense of self-control.

stopping smoking can help improve the quality of your sleep. Smoking can disrupt normal sleep patterns and lead to insomnia; however, stopping smoking can help improve the quality of your sleep.

Quitting smoking can help lower the risk of oral health problems such as gum disease and tooth loss, both of which can be caused by smoking. Quitting smoking can help reduce the risk of these oral health problems.

Stopping the habit of smoking can enhance not just your physical health but also your quality of life in general in a number of different ways, including the ones listed above. If you want to improve not just your physical health but also your mental health and the overall quality of your life, quitting smoking is a smart start in the right direction that you should take.

At that moment, John's habit of smoking spanned more than 20 years at that point. He started smoking when he was a young boy and had made several attempts to quit smoking over the years, but he always found himself going back to cigarettes. He started smoking when he was a young boy. When he was a teenager, he made the decision to start smoking. John, on the other hand, came to the conclusion that he needed to quit smoking for good after years of struggling with his health, having difficulty breathing, and being concerned about the impact that his habit could have on the people he cared about the most.

When I finally kicked my smoking habit, I observed significant changes in my health almost immediately after I had stopped smoking. Within a matter of days, John's sense of smell and taste began to improve, and he became aware of previously unrecognized fragrances and flavors in the food he consumed. He became less self-conscious about the smokey smell that lingered on his clothes and in his hair, and he noticed an increase in the freshness of his breath.

John noticed an increase in the number and intensity of the positive effects that resulted from his decision to quit smoking throughout the course of the subsequent weeks and months. His coughing and the shortness of breath he had been experiencing started to get better, and he was able to exercise and be active without feeling winded. His fingers and toenails had lost their yellowish cast, and his complexion generally appeared to be in better health.

The beneficial changes in John's health and well-being were also noticeable to the rest of his family. They were no longer exposed to secondhand smoke, which lowered the chance of health problems, and they no longer needed to worry about the effects that John's smoking might have on their own health. They were pleased to observe that John was feeling better and happier and were proud of his decision to quit smoking.

John continued to reap the rewards of his decision to quit smoking as the weeks and months passed. He had a sense of success and self-control that helped him feel more confident in other aspects of his life, and he saved money that he had previously spent on cigarettes. He also stopped smoking completely. He was able to enjoy spending time with his family and friends without having to worry about the urge to step outside for a smoke break, and as a result, he felt more connected to the world that was happening around him.

John's efforts to quit smoking were not always successful, and there were times when he had to resist the urge to pick up a cigarette again. Despite this, he did not give up and sought assistance from his friends, family, and the medical professionals around him. He became familiar with various coping skills to help him deal with cravings and triggers, and he discovered new interests and activities to participate in so that he would have something to occupy his time.

The Significance Of Kicking The Habit At A Young Age

Quitting smoking at a younger age is associated with a significantly reduced chance of acquiring smoking-related illnesses and health issues as compared to quitting smoking at a later age. It provides the opportunity for the body to gradually mend and recover from the harm caused by smoking, which ultimately results in improvements in pulmonary function, cardiovascular health, and overall well-being.

Quitting smoking at an earlier age is associated with a reduced chance of having major health disorders later in life. This benefit accrues throughout the course of a person's lifetime. These include diseases of the respiratory system (such as chronic obstructive pulmonary disease), abnormalities of the cardiovascular system, a variety of malignancies (particularly lung cancer), and other ailments that are associated to tobacco use.

Health of the Lungs and Lung Function Smoking is harmful to the lungs and can lead to problems that are irreversible. The lungs are able to repair and restore their optimal function if smoking is stopped as early as possible. This has the potential to enhance breathing, expand lung capacity, and lower the risk of developing chronic respiratory problems.

Improved Cardiovascular Health and Lung Capacity Smoking lowers lung capacity and impairs cardiovascular function, both of which are detrimental to cardiovascular health and athletic performance. When individuals quit smoking at a younger age, they are able to improve their levels of fitness and endurance, as well as their general athletic talents.

Academic Performance and Cognitive Development: Smoking has a poor impact on the brain development, memory, and focus of young people, which in turn negatively impacts their cognitive ability. Teenagers who give up smoking can increase their brain function and their academic performance, which in turn can lead to improved educational chances and future success.

Savings on Money Smoking is a costly habit, therefore giving up the habit at a younger age means you will save a large amount of money over the course of your life. The money saved can be put toward the accomplishment of personal goals, the pursuit of education, or the participation in events that have meaning.

Positive Role Modeling: Giving up smoking as a young person offers a positive example for peers, siblings, and future generations. It exhibits perseverance, self-care, and a commitment to one's health, influencing others to make healthier choices and potentially preventing them from starting to smoke.

Advice On Determining When To Stop Working And Making Arrangements For The Change

Setting a quit date and planning for the change can help people quit smoking effectively. Here are some tips for developing a quit date and preparing for the transition:

1. Choose a meaningful date: Choose a meaningful quit date, such as a birthday or wedding, to give the stopping process more importance.

2. Plan: Plan for the quit date by removing cigarettes from home, finding triggers, and planning coping techniques for handling cravings.

3. Consider using nicotine replacement therapy: Nicotine replacement treatment, such as patches, gum, or lozenges, can help handle withdrawal symptoms and lessen cravings. Talk to a

healthcare provider about whether nicotine replacement treatment is proper.

4. Build a support system: Build a support system of friends, family, or a support group to help you stay responsible and provide support during shopping.

5. Practice stress-reducing techniques: Practice stress-reducing techniques, such as exercise, meditation, or deep breathing, to handle worry and anxiety during the shopping process.

6. Celebrate milestones: Celebrate milestones like a day or week without smoking to honor progress and stay encouraged.

7. Stay positive: Stay positive and focus on the benefits of stopping rather than the difficulties of the quitting process

Methods For Breaking The Habit

Quitting smoking might be challenging for some people, but there are a variety of strategies available to assist them. The following are some useful ways for stopping:

1. Quitting smoking "cold turkey" refers to stopping smoking abruptly without utilizing any nicotine replacement therapy or other cessation methods. People who have a lot of motivation and support may find success with this strategy.

2. Nicotine replacement therapy: Nicotine replacement therapy, which may be administered in the form of patches, gum, or lozenges, can assist with the management of withdrawal symptoms and reduce the intensity of

urges. Before beginning any treatment for nicotine replacement, it is necessary to have a conversation with a healthcare professional.

3. medications There are medications available by prescription that can assist with quitting smoking. Some examples of these medications include bupropion and varenicline. Have a discussion about your medical needs with a qualified professional in the field.

4. Counseling: Different types of counseling, such as cognitive-behavioral therapy or motivational interviewing, can assist individuals in developing useful coping strategies and learning how to manage triggers.

5. Support groups Support organizations, such as Nicotine Anonymous, can offer a feeling of

camaraderie as well as assistance while going shopping.

6. Alternative treatments: Some people may find that alternative treatments like as acupuncture or hypnosis help them better manage their urges and feel less stressed.

7. Get regular exercise. Getting regular exercise can help you deal with stress and concern, reduce desires, and enhance your overall health and well-being.

Alternatives in the Real World

When you are experiencing cravings, it may be helpful to engage in physical activities like brisk walking, stretching, or deep breathing to help you concentrate your attention. These activities both produce endorphins and help reduce stress in the body.

Substitutes Taken by Mouth

The habit of smoking with one's mouth open is common among smokers. You can satisfy your need for oral stimulation without resorting to smoking if you chew sugar-free gum, eat carrot sticks, or munch on other nutritious foods that keep your mouth active.

Meditation and a focus on the present moment

Your ability to manage urges and triggers may improve if you engage in mindfulness techniques. Maintaining presence of mind and reducing tension can be accomplished by the practice of deep breathing techniques, meditation, or gradual muscular relaxation.

Putting One's Thoughts to Work

Participating in activities that require concentration and attention is a good way to get your mind off of things. To divert your attention away from smoking, you could try finishing a crossword puzzle, reading a book, or focusing on a creative endeavor.

Interactions with Other People

When cravings strike, it can be helpful to reach out to friends, family, or support groups. Participating in social activities not only provides a welcome distraction but also helps you feel more committed to maintaining your sobriety.

Help from Trained Professionals

Individualized approaches to coping with smoking triggers can be learned through the guidance of counselors, therapists, and smoking cessation programs. Their coaching teaches you helpful skills that you can utilize to get through challenging moments.

In order to successfully quit smoking, one of the most important steps is to recognize one's triggers and habits. If you are aware of your smoking habits, you will be more equipped to choose healthier alternatives that will break the cycle of addiction. Whether through physical activities, mindfulness approaches, or the assistance of a professional, these options arm you with the tools necessary to respond to triggers in ways that support your goals of quitting smoking. Keep in mind that each time you opt for a healthier option, you're moving one step closer to a life in which you won't have to worry about smoking.

A little testament

The joys and triumphs I have had in aiding others to give up smoking are immense. The most precious present was witnessing their radiant eyes and beaming smiles—those of new individuals, more content, self-assured, and full of vitality.

Among the hundreds of testimonies I have gathered over the years, I would like to share a few with you. I have a strong attachment to the first one, Frank; he is a kind man who is committed to the family and is motivated to recover. The meetings occurred two years prior, yet the testimony is dated from 2006. An authentic and impromptu one.

Frank passed away a few years ago, as I regret to inform you, and I wanted to honour him in this book.

Call me Frank [Age] 63 Working as a retiree Title: Give up; things will improve!

Three encounters in total Pre-smoking cigarettes: 50 per day

I knew that smoking may turn on me at any time, so I had to avoid it at all costs. Entering a centre where people quit smoking piqued their intense curiosity: how could they be certain to conquer my instinctive need to start a cigarette employing a methodology? I started using all of the advice right away to detox, unwind, and take my mind off of the still-present recollection of the cigarette. When you look at some of my old pictures next to my current reflection in the mirror, you can see right away that my face is sunken and my body is excessively dry. I was sick, but I was unaware of it at the time. I've done something practical, safe, and efficient to regain a healthy appearance and a lot of money to spend in other ways!

Addicts, if you don't breathe in the harmful chemicals from cigarettes, your complexion will turn pink again; admit it—you look yellow right now! Marc's testimony, a surgeon at Massachusetts Hospital, is another one of which I am really fond. Meetings began on January 31, 2005.

Call me Marc 40 years old Surgical professionals: Headline I made an attempt to demonstrate that it is effective.

I felt no want to smoke at all after our first encounter, thus I was OK without smoking at all! After ten days, I felt something (perhaps discomfort from giving up the cigarette), so I improved my health with the help of the operator's post-treatment check and another meeting. Five months later, another meeting. After a few months, I unintentionally lit a cigar out of enjoyment while travelling with a friend, and I was screwed! I didn't call for help because I thought I could handle the situation on my own, and I kept going after that cigar until I was almost back to where I was. In spite of this, I have stopped contacting the centre for assistance, albeit I am not sure why. They have, however, always made it clear to me that you can get in touch with us whenever and for any cause. We might place a lot of weight on something that you would consider unimportant.

I had another session, and everything is going really well! I will always want and crave this! It's up to me now! It's great that it works! Try it, and you can quit! I promise that if you simply consider giving up, it will stay just a notion! To prove, I gave it a shot, and it works! Start now! Quit! Put the cigarette out of your mind! Fear of gaining weight or anything else is unfounded; they are typically lame justifications. Thousands of others have accomplished their aim, just like Frank and Marc. Many of them required assistance because they lacked the knowledge or skills necessary to succeed. It's your turn now!

Alcohol Is Smoking's Ugly Sibling.

Where I come from, drinking alcohol and smoking go hand in hand. Together, they are a lethal combination that may ruin your life in a variety of ways. Since we all know this, I won't go into specifics. I won't go into detail about my past with alcohol either, but let's just say that my drinking and smoking histories are comparable. Good news: I stopped drinking much more easily than I stopped smoking, and I received a lot more support and recognition for it. I suppose this is because drinking alcohol is widely acknowledged as a social requirement and it is considered admirable to be self-assured enough not to drink while having a wonderful time, whereas smoking is perceived as self-harming and we shouldn't do it. I don't think it's necessary to drink alcohol in order to have a nice time. Since alcohol is poison, it should never be drank in large amounts. It wrecks havoc on society and is bad for the body.

Although people drink for a variety of reasons, when examined more closely, all of them are illusory. It can give you the confidence to approach the girl, but when you do, what rubbish are you talking about? It might ease your tension, but what form of relaxation—more rest or sleep, for example—can it offer that isn't possible to obtain naturally? Some people drink for the fun it brings, but is it really fun to argue while intoxicated with your best friend or partner? Is it enjoyable to get up in the middle of the night to go potty? Is the morning after a hangover enjoyable? Do you enjoy waking up next to your boss? Is it enjoyable to forget how you got home? In my opinion, no.

Similar to smoking, drinking normally starts with a few drinks with friends and gets worse with time. You will need more and more alcohol to achieve the same effects as your body becomes accustomed to it and develops a tolerance to it. Moreover, alcohol is inconsistent; you could have ten beers one evening and be OK, but the following night you might have five and be nakedly dancing in your neighbor's backyard. For the many people who don't know their limitations, it's an extremely risky game.

The largest problem with consuming alcohol, compared to smoking, is that it weakens our ability to exercise self-control and willpower. Because of this, it is incredibly challenging to escape the smoking trap. The common yet harmful belief that "I only smoke when I drink" is another one. With this kind of thinking, you will probably never quit smoking and might even begin drinking in order to smoke, as it happened to me for a long time. I eventually stopped drinking since it didn't improve my life in a way that couldn't be achieved in other ways. It caused me far too many issues and offered no solutions. For many of you, I'm sure, this is the situation.

I woke up one Sunday morning with the worst hangover ever. While working there, my Russian friend and I were sipping vodka. My body hurt all over, and I sobbed silently from despair. Why do I treat myself like this? While living in this normal state, I would constantly wonder. I made a video of myself that morning, begging my sober self to give up alcohol. I talked about how it was making my life way too chaotic and how I felt. I listened to this five-minute audio several times that day while I lay in bed, and something about it made me wonder what I was doing to myself. That night, I resolved to give up alcohol permanently because it was the most prudent course of action. I'd tried cutting back before, but it didn't work since I couldn't stop after a few beers. This time, I was resolved to give up booze for good.

I was a different man after two or three days without alcohol, and I haven't had the need to drink since. I hate to say never to anything, but I don't think I'll ever be an alcoholic again. I have abstained from alcohol for more than six years as of this writing, and it has been one of the best life-altering choices I have ever made.

A few weeks later, I returned from Russia to my home in Ireland. Those who knew me well didn't think I would abstain from alcohol for very long, but they were mistaken. I followed my usual schedule; initially, I merely switched from alcohol to alcohol-free beer (my fave is a German beverage called Erdinger). When my buddies offered me a drink, I would always request a lager without alcohol. When they'd ask me why I wasn't drinking, I'd usually say something like "I'm pregnant." We would chuckle and call it a day. That has persisted ever since. I can drive home and wake up feeling as fresh as a daisy the next morning, and I still have just as much fun, if not more. Back then, I always kept a "blast" of cans available at home if I wasn't out drinking at night. Back then, there was seldom a night when I didn't drink. I gave up and bought bottles of beer without alcohol to replace these cans. If I had been drinking alcohol, I wouldn't have consumed as much of the non-alcoholic beer. I would simply take my time drinking from a couple bottles. I eventually stopped consuming alcohol-free beer at home and now only occasionally have some when I go out.

Although what transpired in Russia may have been a miracle, there are other ways to accomplish the same goal. I am aware of this since some of my friends have given up drinking as a result of my actions, inspiring others to do the same. They must have believed that if I could accomplish it, then so could they. One evening, a friend called and shared his heartbreaking tale with me. He had a lot going on in his life: his wife was divorcing him, he was likely to lose his job, the kids detested him for never being at home, he became angry after drinking, money was tight, and everything was bad for everyone around him. I listened to his cries for assistance and felt sorry for him. I told him my story, telling him that after the first few days, quitting drinking was not as difficult for me. I told him that my biggest regret was not giving it up sooner.

I told him to record all the reasons he had to give up alcohol since it was ruining his life. Mention all you just told me, I said. After that, spend three days being dry. The alcohol will leave your system after three days, at which point you'll wake up each day feeling better and more resilient. Play your recording whenever you sense the need for a drink. Telling people about your goals and challenges is not worth it. Simply carry it out and let your deeds speak for you. You can make amends with your wife and children as you go along. I told her to forget about living in the past and to start over with a fresh perspective on life. That was basically what we talked about.

At first, I stayed in contact with him, but after a week, I started to hear from him less and less. Four years have passed since then, and he is still sober and doing fantastically. His recent divorce from his wife had nothing to do with his drinking. Indeed, he gave me a great wave when I spotted him sprinting on the highways the other day. Five years ago, he would have been rushing to the pub at this very moment.

Choosing A Date To Quit

Choosing a Quit Date: Your Road to a Life Free of Smoke

Smoking has long been considered a social scourge that causes countless health issues and millions of deaths annually. Even with the understanding of the risks, quitting smoking is extremely difficult for many people. Selecting a date to quit is frequently the key to a successful withdrawal. The importance of setting a quit date, strategies for achieving it, and ways to stay committed to your smoke-free journey will all be covered in this article.

The Importance of Deciding on a Quitting Date

Selecting a stop date is an important step in the quitting process, even though it might seem simple. It helps you mentally be ready for the journey ahead and serves as a concrete expression of your intention to change. This is the reason it's vital:

1. Psychological Preparation: There are psychological as well as physical aspects to quitting smoking. By choosing a stop date, you allow yourself time to prepare mentally for this significant change in your life. You can start to visualise a world free of smokers and develop an optimistic mindset.

2. Accountability: You take responsibility for your decision to stop smoking when you set a quit date. It turns into an objective to work towards, which raises the possibility that you will honour your promise. You may feel obligated to your fans as well as to yourself.

3. Planning: In the event that you give up one day, you can have your plan ready. You can gather information, read up on different quitting methods, and talk to your loved ones about your decision. By

organising, you can deal with potential obstacles and triggers before they arise.

How to Pick the Ideal Date for Your Quit

Making the right decision regarding the stop date will determine how well you do. To ensure that the day you choose will improve your chances of quitting smoking, consider the following suggestions:

1. Individual Importance:

Choose a day, such as your birthday, your anniversary, or the start of a new month, that holds particular significance for you. As a result, the date will be more memorable and you might feel more driven.

2. Stress-Free Period: Refrain from picking a quit date if your life is really busy. In times of extreme stress, it could be harder to resist the urge to smoke. Pick a moment when you feel calm and collected.

3. Health Milestone: Consider tying your cessation date to a tangible accomplishment. Establish a deadline for quitting by using a recent health concern brought on by smoking, for example.

4. Seek Professional Advice:

If you're unsure about the best time to quit, speak with a medical professional or a counsellor for quitting smoking. They might offer guidance that is specific to your situation.

Go Forward And Present A Goal.

According to David Markman, a brain research instructor at the College of Texas and author of "Brilliant Change: Five Devices to Make New and Supportable Propensities in Yourself As well as Other People," the persuasive framework is a collection of cerebrum components that achieve goals. The "Go framework," as defined by Markman, is a collection of mental constructs that your inspiring framework uses to motivate behaviour. The "Stop framework" aims to prevent you from giving in to temptations or doing things you would prefer not to do.

Therefore, while contemplation can be a remarkable process to silence the Go capabilities, goal-setting is essential to reimagining that framework and advancing. You can't eat potato chips and sew at the same time, so look into ways to rebuild the Go structure by performing other activities, he suggested. Either way, you're continuously applying the brake to the Stop element.

It also helps to state such goals in a positive manner. Markman suggests saying "I will carry on with life as a nonsmoker" instead of "I will quit smoking," which is a negative statement intended to stop a way of behaviour.

Establish a plan.

Christine Whelan teaches and directs research in the Purchaser Science department at the School of Human Nature, College of Wisconsin-Madison. "Discretion is a muscle that gets strong(er) when you practise it," she explains. "When we make the effort to abstain from smoking or consuming foods high in calories, we might succeed throughout the day."

However, if that muscle is required to operate continuously, it also becomes exhausted, according to Whelan. It's important to come to an agreement before our defences are compromised in order to prevent the inevitable jams that inevitably arise, she argues. "That is the point at which we are the most drastically averse to have the option to apply restraint." And those might be the moments when we feel excited, angry, hopeless, or exhausted.

Clearly state what you will do in place of the inclination, such as taking a walk or biting your gum, and indicate the time and location of the activities. According to Markman, saying "I won't smoke" is insufficient. "Make beneficial ways of behaving simple and unfortunate ways of behaving hard." He suggests starting with throwing of the crisis pack of smokes or the snack food supplies scattered throughout the house.

According to Whelan, it's also crucial to identify a substitute for the "reward" that you expect from your behaviour. Could a hot shower or a conversation with a friend suffice as a kind of comfort instead of a bowl of frozen yoghurt? To put oneself in a good position, the arrangement needs to be clear and made in front of those minutes.

It will also provide your mind with a break. "At the point when you're confronted with a circumstance requiring a poise difficulty, you will be prepared with an elective method for taking care of it," states Bunny, "rather than expecting to burn through extra mental energy to think of a choice on the spot." Let the world in and solicit feedback. Benefit from the common difficulties; it can serve as a powerful source of motivation. Inform those you care about about your goals and plans so they may participate in the accountability conversation."According to Whelan, obligations that are confidential are more susceptible to modification than those that are public. "Public obligations to adapt are becoming increasingly 'exorbitant.'" You would prefer not to look foolish in front of your friends, and you might also get their backing."

Slow Disengagement

For many people, giving up smoking can be a daunting and challenging job. A smoking cessation strategy that may prove beneficial for certain individuals is the gradual detachment method. With this method, the smoker's daily cigarette intake is progressively decreased until they are able to give up entirely.

The first step in the gradual separation approach is to decide how many fewer cigarettes you want to smoke each day. For instance, on the first day of trying to stop, the target would be to cut the smoker's usual daily cigarette intake down to 39 cigarettes from 40. The objective would be to cut it down to 38 smokes the following day, and so on. By progressively cutting back on cigarettes smoked, the smoker can acclimatise to smoking less and less, which lessens the likelihood of experiencing the psychological and physical withdrawal symptoms associated with abrupt stopping.

When employing the progressive separation technique, it's critical to have a support network in place. A friend or loved one can assist hold the smoker accountable for their success and offer support and encouragement throughout the process. You may give them a call every day to congratulate them and kindly remind them to stay on course.

It's crucial to remember that you should only use this technique on someone you genuinely detest and who is open to using it with you. Reaching the objective of quitting entirely may take several weeks or even months due to the gradual nature of the separation process. The advantages of stopping smoking, however, exceed the time and effort needed to do so.

Finding the smoking cessation strategy that works best for you is crucial because quitting is a personal experience. Although it might not be suitable for everyone, gradual detachment might be a useful strategy for certain smokers. Before quitting, it's crucial to discuss the best course of action with your healthcare professional and to have a strategy in place. Recall that stopping smoking is a process that calls for perseverance and resolve, but the rewards to your health and wellbeing make the effort worthwhile.

Exercise and physical activity

Exercise and physical activity are important for helping people quit smoking and for sustaining a healthy, smoke-free lifestyle. Regular physical activity has many advantages that can help you in your road to quit smoking. Here are some ways that exercise and physical activity can help you stop smoking:

1. Craving Management: Exercise helps lessen cravings and control the symptoms of nicotine withdrawal. Exercise allows you to divert your attention from smoking when a craving strikes. Exercise causes the brain to release endorphins, which are naturally

occurring chemicals that improve mood by boosting wellbeing and lessening the severity of cravings.

2. Stress Reduction: Giving up smoking may make you feel more stressed. Frequent exercise relieves stress by lowering anxiety, elevating happiness, and encouraging relaxation. Exercise facilitates the release of tension and increases endorphin production, both of which can reduce stress and improve general wellbeing.

3. Better Lung Function: Smoking impairs respiratory health and destroys the lungs. Aerobic activities that promote lung capacity, cardiovascular fitness, and general lung function

include jogging, cycling, swimming, and brisk walking. After stopping smoking, regular exercise can help the respiratory system mend and recuperate.

4. Weight Management: People who stop smoking frequently worry about gaining weight. Engaging in regular physical activity can aid in weight management by increasing metabolism, burning calories, and constructing lean muscle mass. Including cardiovascular and strength training activities in your regimen can help you achieve your weight loss or maintenance objectives.

5. Improves General Health: When it comes to enhancing general health, giving up smoking and exercising go

hand in hand. Exercise helps strengthen bones, improve circulation, lower blood pressure, lower the risk of heart disease, and boost immunity. These advantages lessen the health hazards connected with smoking and enhance your general well-being.

6. Increased Vitality and Energy: Engaging in regular physical activity increases stamina and energy levels, which facilitates everyday activities and an active lifestyle. You might feel more energised and like you're in better shape as your fitness level rises, which will give you more incentive to keep quitting smoking.

7. Healthier Coping Mechanism: As a coping strategy, exercise is a better option than smoking. Physical activity provides a healthy outlet for managing emotions, relieving tension, and encouraging a good outlook in stressful or emotional situations, as opposed to reaching for a cigarette.

The following advice should be taken into consideration when adding exercise to your quitting journey:

Start out slowly: Start with low-impact exercises if you've never exercised before or have been inactive, and gradually increase the duration and intensity over time.

Pick out pursuits that spark your interest: Discover pursuits that you take pleasure in and that correspond to your individual interests, such as going for a stroll, dancing, cycling, swimming, or competing in team sports. This raises the likelihood that you will continue to adhere to your fitness plan.

Develop it into a routine: Aim for at least 150 minutes of aerobic exercise per week at a moderate intensity or 75 minutes of exercise per week at a high intensity. In addition, strive to participate in muscle-strengthening exercises at least twice per week.

Maintain your uniformity: Create a timetable that includes time for regular exercise and make it a priority to include some form of physical activity in each day's or week's agenda.

Seek the help of your peers: If you want to make exercise more pleasurable and benefit from the support and accountability of others while doing so, consider working out with a friend, enrolling in a fitness class, or taking part in other group activities.

Before beginning any type of exercise program, it is important to discuss your health with your primary care physician, particularly if you have any preexisting health conditions or concerns. They are able to give individualized advice and suggestions based on the specifics of your situation.

Keep in mind that including regular physical activity and exercise into your life not only assists you in your path to quit smoking but also improves overall health, well-being, and an improved quality of life.

Personalized Approach: In the end, the decision to take nicotine replacement therapies (NRTs) is mainly dependent on the person. Some people find them to be extremely helpful in the management of cravings and withdrawal symptoms, while others favor a strategy that does not involve nicotine. You should discuss your health, preferences, and objectives with a trained medical practitioner in order to establish whether or not NRTs are a treatment choice that is appropriate for you.

You can make an educated decision that improves your chances of successfully quitting smoking and transitioning to a healthier lifestyle if you consider the benefits and drawbacks of nicotine replacement therapies (NRTs) and customize your approach to meet the specific requirements of your situation.

How to Handle Your Cravings and the Symptoms of Nicotine Withdrawal

Managing the physical and mental symptoms of nicotine withdrawal while avoiding cravings is one of the most difficult aspects of quitting smoking. You should expect to experience these intense feelings as a natural part of the process of quitting smoking; but, with the help of appropriate tactics, you will be able to manage them effectively and emerge stronger on your journey to a life free of smoking.

A Comprehendion of the Cravings and Symptoms of Withdrawal

Your body reacts negatively when it is deprived of nicotine, causing cravings as well as withdrawal symptoms. They usually reach their height within the first few days after quitting, and then they steadily decrease over the course of time. Irritability, restlessness, an increased hunger, difficulty concentrating, and mood fluctuations are all common signs of bipolar disorder.

Techniques for Overcoming Cravings and Coping with Withdrawal Symptoms:

1. Engage in constructive self-talk by exchanging negative thoughts with affirmations of a positive nature. Remind yourself of the benefits you'll reap from stopping as well as the reasons you decided to quit in the first place.

2. Distraction Techniques: Participate in activities that cause a shift in your attention, such as reading, working out, doing puzzles, or spending time with people you care about.

3. Practice deep breathing exercises to help relax your thoughts and lessen worry. These exercises can be found here. Deeply inhale for the count of four, hold for the same amount of time, and then exhale for the same amount of time.

4.Keep Your Hydration Levels Up: Water helps wash toxins out of your system and can reduce the severity of some withdrawal symptoms if you drink it often.

5.Eat Healthier Snacks: If you find that you have an increased appetite, try keeping some nutritious snacks on hand. Consuming plenty of fruits, vegetables, and grains in their entire form can assist in warding off excessive eating.

6.Physical Activity: Endorphins, which can assist boost your mood and help you manage cravings, are released into your system when you regularly engage in physical activity.

7. Chew gum or candy that does not include sugar: You can satisfy the oral fixation that comes along with smoking by chewing gum or sucking on sugar-free candies. This will give you a sensory distraction at the same time.

Nicotine Replacement Therapies (NRTs): Think about utilizing nicotine replacement therapies (NRTs), such as nicotine gum or patches, to ease withdrawal symptoms while gradually reducing the amount of nicotine you take in.

9. Mindfulness and meditation: Incorporating mindfulness practices into your daily routine can help you remain present in the moment, better manage stress, and steer clear of being fixated on cravings.

10. When you feel a hunger coming on, remind yourself to wait a few minutes before giving in to it. This is the "delay technique." During this period, you may notice that the strength of the urge begins to lessen.

11. Give Yourself Positive Reinforcement: Reward Yourself When You Succeed 11. Give yourself positive reinforcement when you succeed in overcoming urges and completing milestones. As a reward for your hard work and continued improvement, do something fun for yourself.

12. Support System: Lean on your support network for understanding and encouragement and use it as a support system. Talking about your difficulties with someone who understands what you're going through can bring a great deal of relief.

13. Seek Professional Assistance: If you find that the urges to smoke and the withdrawal symptoms are too much to handle, you should seriously consider getting help from a healthcare provider

or a counselor who is skilled in helping people quit smoking.

1. Do not attempt to cut from the final cigarette to the first cigarette in reverse, as this is not the correct way to do the technique.

As a result, by the time you find out about the method, a small voice in the back of your mind may ask you, "Okay, it's all about quitting that cigarette in that time; why shouldn't I quit it in reverse order?" If this is the case, you will have learned enough about the strategy. For instance, "Why shouldn't I quit the cigarette that I smoke after dinner at 8.30 pm as 1st and the last but one at 6.30 pm as 2nd and why shouldn't I continue in the reverse order?" is a reasonable question to ask.

The important thing for you to realize is that the purpose of this method is to condition your body to function normally in the absence of the more than

7,000 chemicals that are found in cigarettes for as long as possible, beginning as soon as you open your eyes in the morning until the end of the 28-day period, so that it can be prepared to do so for the rest of your life, regardless of the number of years involved. Regarding myself, I have been able to abstain from smoking for more than 15 years now, even without the slightest desire to light up. Because my body has been properly taught to tolerate, and trained to give up, those toxins, I don't even get the want to smoke when I'm in a situation where there are other people smoking around me. Therefore, you shouldn't try to perform the procedure backwards.

2. If you are someone who drinks alcohol on a regular basis, you should refrain from consuming alcohol during this period of 28 days even if you normally

use alcohol. Because drinking makes it far more likely that you will smoke more cigarettes, the likelihood of you doing so increases when you drink. In addition to that, there is the danger of disrupting this path of quitting. For instance, on days 22-24, if you have successfully quit smoking your eighth cigarette at 5.30 p.m., but then you go to a party, start drinking at 7 p.m., and consume an additional 4-5 cigarettes, your journey will be derailed because of the drinking and smoking.

Therefore, after you have begun this voyage and have succeeded in giving up the first three to five cigarettes, continue with the flow and finish the journey without any hiccups. Avoid getting involved in anything that could make your journey more difficult. Because of this, we saw in Chapter 6 how the environment plays an essential role in this journey. Because of this, it is crucial to ask your family and friends to help you in this journey. This is why we saw in Chapter 6 how the environment plays an important role in this journey.

The Prevalence Of The Stigma Is Astounding

Many people decide to stop smoking because they are unable to deal with the way society treats them; nevertheless, this is not a particularly compelling reason to do so. At this point in time, culture, technology, the media, and individual people are all aware of the hazards posed by cannabis and cigarettes, and they preach about it.

In contrast to what you might believe, some people who smoke, including most likely yourself, do not take pleasure in being condemned. Some people interpret it as a message to quit smoking for good, while others may see it as a call to be more discreet with their smoking. Sometimes, in addition to the stigma, there are other surrounding causes, such as the desire to spend more time at a social gathering of loved ones without feeling the need to use a stick.

Mindfulness of one's health

Do you have any idea what takes place when you inhale deeply from a cigarette and exhale smoke? Your resting heart rate and blood pressure both decrease, which, over the course of time, could cause permanent harm to your heart. Also, research has shown that smoking cigarettes is responsible for the development of lung cancer in 90 percent of patients who have the disease.

Some people who used to smoke have given up the habit after having a sudden epiphany about the negative effects smoking has on one's health and making the conscious decision to give up the habit. This realization is possibly sparked by a brand-new and exciting cause to live, such as a new baby or a new job, or, as my buddy indicated earlier, a need to be close to family. Both of these scenarios have the potential to bring about this epiphany.

Consider the following: is it possible for someone who is battling respiratory disorders to enjoy activities such as running, hiking, or any other pleasurable activity with their loved ones.

Hearing about other people's triumphs in kicking the habit of smoking

It's true that one of the primary draws of smoking is the enhancement of one's mood, right? But there's also another sensation that comes with quitting nicotine, which is the component in cigarettes that causes addiction (we'll talk more about it later). This sensation is referred to as relief, and in certain cases, freedom. After listening to the life-changing experiences of former smokers who were similar to them, some people make the decision to give up the habit. When you read stories of people who got rid of weird wrinkles on their face, black lips, stained teeth, or flat lips, and how doing so altered their self-perception and confidence, it piques your interest, and you begin to fantasize that you could achieve a similar outcome for yourself. A smoker's desire for a better life and the possibility of one day being an inspiration to others are two of the primary motivating factors that ultimately lead to the decision to give up smoking.

If you fit into this category, don't worry about it.

Maintaining Success Over The Long Term While Trying To Avoid Failure

The decision to stop smoking is a huge step forward, but this is only the beginning of the journey. To live a life free from smoking, it is essential to continue to be successful over the long term and to take steps to avoid relapsing. This chapter will highlight the necessity of building continuing motivation and celebrating accomplishments in order to remain smoke-free. It will also examine common triggers and high-risk situations for relapse, present tactics for controlling cravings and preventing relapse in hard settings, and explore common triggers and high-risk situations for relapse.

A. Being Aware of the Typical Triggers and Dangerous Circumstances That Can Lead to Relapse

It is crucial to know and be aware of common triggers and high-risk scenarios that can tempt you to return to smoking in order to prevent relapse. This will help you avoid returning to smoking. You will be able to successfully traverse these triggers if you first identify them and then build techniques to deal with them. Stressful conditions, social situations and pressure from peers, emotional states, environmental cues, and the use of alcohol or drugs are examples of common triggers. The ability to recognize these triggers gives you the power to respond appropriately and prevent future relapses.

B. Strategies for Managing Cravings and Preventing Relapse when Confronted with Difficult Circumstances

The key to having a smoke-free life is learning how to control your desires and avoid going back to smoking. The following are some strategies that can assist you when confronted with difficult circumstances:

Engage in a mentally stimulating and physically beneficial activity to take your mind off of the urges to snack. The strength of cravings can be mitigated by engaging in activities such as physical exercise, listening to music, or following a hobby.

Perform exercises of slow, deep breathing and relaxation in order to: Through the practice of relaxation techniques and exercises that focus on deep breathing, you can bring your mind and body to a state of calm. Imagine yourself as a content non-smoker, and put your attention on the many advantages of kicking the habit.

Make use of affirmations positive: You should repeat positive affirmations that support your commitment to living a life free of smoking. Remind yourself of your inner fortitude and resolve to win the battle against your urges.

When you feel that your desires are getting out of control, it is important to reach out to those who can help you. Encouragement, guidance, and a sense of accountability can all be provided by friends, family, or support groups.

Maintain a mindful attitude: Focus your attention on the here and now and examine your cravings without passing judgment on them. Recognize that the urges to indulge are only fleeting and remind yourself that they will pass.

Change your daily habits: Find routines or habits that are related with smoking, and then make changes to those routines or habits to sever the connection. Quit smoking and try one of the many healthy alternatives available, such as going for a walk or participating in a mindful activity.

Make use of nicotine replacement therapy (NRT): If you find yourself in need of it, try making use of nicotine replacement therapy (NRT), such as nicotine gum or patches, in order to manage your cravings and progressively diminish your dependence on nicotine. For advice and direction, speak with a qualified healthcare expert.

The Phenomenon Of Putting On Weight After Giving Up Smoking

It is a big accomplishment that can have a substantial impact on a person's health and well-being if they are able to give up smoking. However, quitting smoking can also be associated with a side effect that is less desirable for many smokers, and that is weight gain. In this chapter, we will discuss the topic of gaining weight after quitting smoking. Specifically, we will investigate the reasons why this occurs, the impact it might have, and the techniques that can help prevent it.

Nicotine is a stimulant that boosts heart rate and metabolism, which may be one of the primary reasons why former smokers experience weight gain after giving up the habit. The body of a smoker who stops smoking will go through a period of adjustment as it adjusts to life without nicotine. During this time, the metabolism will slow down, which may result in the smoker gaining weight. Additionally, quitting smoking can lead to changes in eating patterns. This is because former smokers may turn to food as a means of coping with stress and anxiety as well as cravings for cigarettes.

Putting on weight after giving up smoking can be a big obstacle, as it has the potential to negatively affect a person's sense of pride and self-confidence, as well as lead to emotions of anger and disappointment. The accumulation of excess fat in a person's body raises their risk of developing a number of diseases and disorders, including diabetes, cancer, and cardiovascular disease. This makes it possible for weight growth to have a detrimental effect on a person's health.

On the other hand, putting on weight after giving up smoking is not an unavoidable consequence, and there are methods that can assist in preventing it. The most important thing is to form good routines, such as maintaining a nutritious diet, being physically active on a regular basis, and learning appropriate coping mechanisms for dealing with stress and worry. In addition, smokers who are concerned about their weight gain should consult with their healthcare provider, as this person is in the best position to offer individualized counsel and assistance.

In conclusion, giving up smoking is a great victory that can have a considerable influence on the health and well-being of a person. However, for some former smokers, giving up the habit might be complicated by the additional issue of putting on weight. Smokers can kick the habit, avoid gaining weight, and start reaping the numerous benefits of a smoke-free life all at the same time if they commit to adopting healthy behaviors and seek advice from healthcare professionals.

The Repercussions Of Smoking, Both Physiologically And Mentally

In the beginning... A huge toll is taken not just on your physical health but also on your mental and emotional well-being when you smoke. It is crucial to your own motivation to quit smoking that you have a thorough understanding of the myriad impacts that smoking has on both your body and mind. This chapter will discuss the damaging effects of tobacco on both the body and the mind, providing light on how important it is to kick this unhealthy habit.

1.1 The Systems Involved in Breathing

The effects of smoking on one's respiratory system are significant and substantial. Toxic chemicals found in cigarette smoke cause irreparable damage to the airways and the fragile lung tissue when they are inhaled. This damage, if left unchecked, can, over time, result in chronic illnesses such as chronic bronchitis and emphysema, as well as an increased chance of developing lung cancer. In addition, smoking makes respiratory symptoms, such as coughing, wheezing, and shortness of breath, significantly worse.

1.2 The Heart and the Blood Vessels

Tobacco smoke contains compounds that are known to cause direct damage to the cardiovascular system. The chance of developing cardiovascular disease, stroke, and peripheral artery disease is increased when a person smokes. Toxic chemicals in cigarettes can cause blood arteries to constrict, which results in decreased blood flow and an increased risk of blood clots. Smoking also causes an increase in heart rate and blood pressure, both of which place additional strain on the heart.

1.3 Surface Area and General Appearance

The appearance and health of your skin will suffer, as will the natural aging process, if you continue to smoke. Tobacco smoke contains substances that constrict blood vessels and reduce the amount of oxygen and nutrients that reach the skin. This can lead to the skin aging prematurely, developing wrinkles, becoming dry, and having a poor complexion. In addition, smoking raises the likelihood of acquiring skin disorders such as psoriasis and cancer of the skin.

The psychological effects of smoking are discussed in Section 2.

2.1 Addictive Behaviors and Physical Dependence

Not only does smoking produce a physical addiction, but it also produces a psychological addiction. When a someone attempts to quit smoking, they will experience cravings as well as withdrawal symptoms due to the nicotine that is found in tobacco products, which creates a cycle of dependence. Because smoking is addictive, people who partake in the habit may experience feelings of helplessness, worry, and frustration as a result of their dependence on the habit.

2.2 Implications for Psychological Health

The detrimental effects of smoking on one's mental health are severe. According to the findings of numerous studies, there is a close connection between smoking and illnesses of mental health such as anxiety and depression. Individuals may first turn to smoking as a means of coping with stress or regulating their emotions; however, the long-term consequences of nicotine can make these issues worse and lead to a damaging cycle of dependency on the substance.

2.3 The Influence on One's Quality of Life

Your whole quality of life can suffer significantly if you are a smoker. The consistent contact with hazardous substances found in cigarettes raises the danger of a wide range of diseases and health difficulties, which in turn leads to a decrease in physical endurance, an increase in weariness, and restrictions on the kinds of activities that may be done. The social stigma associated with smoking and the requirement to remove oneself from social contexts in order to light up can have an effect on relationships and social interactions, which in turn can have an effect on one's wellbeing.

Realizing how destructive smoking is to your health and well-being requires first having a solid understanding of the habit's impacts, both physiological and psychological. A considerable number of facets of your life are negatively impacted by smoking, including your respiratory and cardiovascular systems, your skin, and your mental and emotional well-being. By being aware of these consequences, you give yourself the power to take the measures required to quit smoking and restore your health as well as your joy in life. In the following chapters, we will delve into natural aids, techniques, and strategies to support your quest to quit smoking and improve your general well-being. These will be discussed in detail.

The Numerous Advantages Of Giving Up Smoking

Stopping the use of tobacco products is one of the most important steps you can take to enhance both your physical health and your general well-being. In this chapter, we will discuss the numerous advantages of giving up smoking. These advantages might act as incentive to help you maintain your commitment to a lifestyle free of smoking.

Advantages to One's Health

Giving up smoking will almost immediately bring about improvements to your physical health. The following is a list of some of the most important health benefits:

Enhanced capacity of the lungs: As soon as you stop smoking, your lung function starts to improve, which makes it easier to engage in physical activities and reduces the sensation of being short of breath.

Quitting smoking helps improve the immune system's ability to fight off infections, which lowers the chance of respiratory infections such as bronchitis and pneumonia. Quitting smoking also lessens the severity of respiratory infections that do occur.

Quitting smoking is associated with a considerable reduction in the chance of developing heart disease, as well as lowering the risk of experiencing a heart attack and having a stroke. The risk of heart disease lowers by half during the first year after quitting smoking, and after 15 years, it is comparable to the risk that a non-smoker would have.

Quitting smoking reduces the risk of several different types of cancer, including lung, mouth, and throat cancer, as well as cancer of the esophagus, bladder, and pancreas. After ten years of not smoking, a person's risk of developing lung cancer lowers by fifty percent.

Increased chances of conceiving a healthy pregnancy and child Quitting smoking can boost fertility in both men and women, which in turn increases the likelihood of the pregnancy and child being born healthy.

A nonsmoker can expect to live roughly 10 years longer than a smoker on average. Smokers have a shorter life expectancy. Stopping smoking at any point in your life can add years to your overall lifespan.

Advantages to One's Body

Quitting smoking will not only enhance your health in the long run, but it will also provide you with a number of instant physical benefits.

stopping smoking can help restore your sense of taste and smell, allowing you to appreciate food and aromas to a greater extent than before. Smoking affects the taste buds and olfactory receptors, but stopping can help restore these senses.

Enhanced state of oral health Quitting smoking not only improves the appearance of your teeth but also decreases the likelihood that you will suffer from gum disease, tooth loss, and bad breath.

Better care for the skin and hair: The aging process is sped up by smoking, which in turn causes premature wrinkles and a dull complexion. Quitting smoking can increase the flexibility of the skin, lessen the appearance of wrinkles, and promote healthier, more radiant skin overall. Quitting can also improve the health of your hair and lessen the risk of premature graying and hair loss.

Advantages of One's Bank Account

Depending on how much you smoked and the price of cigarettes in your region, the financial benefits of quitting smoking can be significant:

Spending less cash: Consider how much money you will save over time if you factor in the amount of money you previously spent on cigarettes and do the math. This can be an extremely effective way to motivate oneself, and it can also be put toward funding other personal goals or interests.

Insurance premium discounts: If you are a nonsmoker, you may be eligible for insurance premium discounts across the board, including health, life, and disability insurance. These discounts could save you hundreds or even thousands of dollars over the course of your life.

Advantages to One's Social and Emotional Life

Giving up smoking can lead to a number of social and emotional benefits, all of which can contribute to an improvement in a person's overall well-being:

Quitting smoking successfully can offer you a sense of accomplishment, which can lead to improvements in both one's self-esteem and one's level of confidence.

Improved interpersonal connections: If you want to improve your relationships with friends, family, and coworkers who may have been negatively impacted by your smoking habits or the health risks linked with them, quitting smoking is a good place to start.

Modelingbehavior that is beneficial: Your decision to give up smoking will serve as a positive example for your children, friends, and loved ones, and may encourage them to make decisions that are better for their health.

Positive Effects on the Environment

How To Remain Smoke-Free Once You Have Quit

You're able to take the initial step toward quitting because of an unwavering passion. Having the ability to swim against the current makes you one of the fortunate individuals alive. You've stood out from the crowd by demonstrating a strong sense of self-determination among your friends and family.

Is there any manner you would want to use that in that situation, once you have managed to answer the most significant call of your life?

Is there anything that can ever match your mental fortitude? Would you even attempt to make a fool of yourself in front of those closest to you? What kind of an impression do you provide your children?

You struggle with memory loss and indecision. Maybe even show that smoking is so beneficial that it is impossible for anyone to give it up. Keep in mind that your spouse and kids look up to you at all times. Lastly, we have nothing at all to say if you choose to take on the risks of losing your standing in both the family and society. But if you choose to follow the most noble course and stay put, we can support you to the fullest extent possible. This chapter will help you achieve your desired but unconventional aim.

from forgetfulness and a lack of discernment. Alternatively, you may even prove that smoking is so necessary that quitting is impossible. Remind yourself that your spouse and children look up to you.

Moreover, should you choose to assume the risk of losing your social and familial position, we are at a loss for words. However, if you decide to stick with the honorable decision to stay put, we will help you as much as we can, and this chapter will be a big help in helping you accomplish your desired but unusual goal.

Because smoking has subjected your body and mind to the allure of nicotine, you may find yourself drawn to situations and people once more. But one needs to control these unwanted tendencies.

Because the mind controls everything with an iron grasp, one more puff could send you slipping back to where you started, even years later.

The greatest divide in the modern society is awareness.

When two people are having a sexual connection, neither one of them is aware of the feelings that the other is experiencing. The mental health benefits that can be gained by viewing blue movies are mostly unknown to adolescents. The group that is tasked with following the missing person is NOT informed of the dangers and risks that come with being in an unfamiliar region with an unpredictable environment. It is not yet common knowledge how addiction to drugs affects both the physical and mental health of today's younger population. Perhaps you didn't give much thought to the consequences of smoking when you took that first drag from your cigarette. You have finally come to realize how detrimental smoking is to your health because of the high cost. Since you have already taken the first step toward maturity by quitting, the next stage is to become aware of the likely occurrences that may cause you to go back into old habits. It's possible that we've conceived of some generically applicable overarching ideas or triggering occurrences. A mind that is already predisposed to smoking is stimulated further when it is among other people who are smoking. Therefore, you should start avoiding the smoking areas. We are grateful to the government for requiring businesses to designate a separate area for people to smoke. Start going to eateries that don't allow smoking. Taking vitamins by mouth smoking is a typical misconception held by smokers; hence, you need to exclude both from your daily routine for a period of time until both your body and mind begin to experience the benefits of quitting smoking.

The challenge lies in the fact that in order to light a cigarette, an individual must make use of both of his hands, whereas those who have received specialized training need just one. Why don't you keep your hands occupied by holding a pencil and a rubber at the same time? The habit of smoking is quite easy to pick up. Therefore, it is important to avoid hanging out with smokers and to ask your pals not to light up in front of you. There are certain times of the day that are ideal for smoking, such as after tea or lunch, when you are at your most vulnerable to being provoked. Why don't you try different methods to distract yourself when you're at these crossroads in your life? It would be in your best advantage. You might also plan your job such that you have a lot on your plate after lunch. This would keep you from getting distracted. As a way to keep yourself engaged, you could try your hand at making toffee or churns.

A large number of fake cigarettes, such as Yixing No Smoking Herbal "Cigarettes," have been developed. These "cigarettes" are believed to be less hazardous to one's health than a standard cigarette, and they also provide the same scent as a real cigarette. When one has quit smoking and has reached these stages, these are the things that others prescribe.

Because we have never made an effort to verify the legitimacy of the chemical components that it contains or the effect that it has on smokers, we do not suggest using them. The reasoning behind this is straightforward: if you begin working on this project, the total may reach 20 once more within a period of five to seven years. It seems as if we are travelling in circles, with the exception that we have deceived our thoughts into believing that we have moved on to a less destructive addiction. To us, a cigarette is a cigarette, and even addiction to anything that even remotely resembles a cigarette should be absolutely prohibited, as our feeble minds would again try to find for solace and create explanations while we succumb to another form of addiction. To us, a cigarette is a cigarette. To light a cigarette often requires the use of both hands, however those who are particularly competent can do it with just one hand. Why not keep your hands busy by holding a pencil and a rubber at the same time? One of the most addictive behaviors is smoking. Therefore, stay away from places where people are smoking and encourage your friends to refrain from lighting up in front of you. When you are most likely to get provoked, such as right after lunch or tea, smoking is a good activity to engage in during those specific times. Why don't you try out some other ways to differentiate yourself during times like these when it would be in your best favor to do so? You might also organize your chores in such a way that there will be enough work for you to perform after lunch. To maintain interest, one could try their hand at toffees or "churns."

There have been several attempts made to create fake cigarettes that mimic the aroma of real tobacco products. One example of this is the Yixing No Smoking Herbal "Cigarettes," which are promoted as being safer than traditional cigarettes. After you have successfully given up smoking, many people recommend utilizing them. As a result of the fact that we have never made an effort to ascertain the authenticity of its chemical components or the effect that it has on smokers, we are unable to offer you any advice regarding their use. Given the simplicity of the reasoning, it is possible that the number will be back at 20 within five to seven years from the time you begin working on this issue. It's as if we're going in circles as we fool ourselves into thinking that we've found a less harmful addiction. To us, there is no difference between a cigarette and the addiction that it causes.

Anything that even vaguely resembles a cigarette should be made illegal because our feeble minds will once again try to find solace in it and use it to excuse our relapsing into another addiction.

If you give in to your appetites, though, it can make you question whether or not you are a self-assured person in the first place. Provocations will come and go.

Finding It Difficult To Kick The Habit While You're Pregnant?

Protecting your unborn kid from the dangers of secondhand smoke is one of the most important things you can do to give your child the greatest possible start in life. It is never too late to kick the habit of smoking, despite the fact that giving up smoking can be challenging.

Because each cigarette contains more than 4,000 chemicals, many of which are toxic, smoking while pregnant is detrimental to the health of the unborn child. If you smoke cigarettes, it may be more difficult for your baby to take in the oxygen that it requires. As a direct consequence of this, each time you smoke, their heart rate must increase.

The several advantages of giving up smoking during pregnancy

If you want to start providing immediate benefits to both you and your unborn kid, you should give up smoking. Carbon monoxide is one of the potentially hazardous gases and substances that will be expelled from your body. When you finally kick the habit, you will lower your risk of experiencing complications throughout pregnancy and labor and delivery.

You will almost certainly have a more pleasant pregnancy and a more pleasant offspring as a result.

You will make it less likely that the baby will be stillborn.

Your child has a lower risk of being created at an untimely stage and hence of having to deal with the breathing, caring for, and medical concerns that typically accompany premature birth.

There is a decreased likelihood that your child may be delivered into the world with a low birth weight.

The fact that smokers' newborns are often lighter than other babies can make labor and delivery more difficult for the mother. For example, it will be difficult for them to maintain their body temperature, and they will almost certainly become ill.

The risk of sudden infant death syndrome (SIDS), sometimes known as "bunk death," will be decreased as a result of your actions.

Putting an end to your smoking habit right now will be beneficial to your child in the long run as well. Children whose parents smoke have an increased risk of developing asthma and other serious illnesses, and these children are more likely to require hospital treatment.

It is in your best interest to give up smoking as soon as possible. Even if you quit during the final several weeks of your pregnancy, this will still be beneficial for both you and your unborn child.

How to kick the habit while you're expecting a baby. It is in your best interest to give up smoking as soon as you possibly can. Your child's oxygen intake will immediately improve just one day after you make even the slightest effort to quit smoking. Additionally, your mood will improve.

Methods for giving up smoking

Seek assistance.

Women who receive therapy to help them quit smoking have a quit rate that is forty percent higher than that of other pregnant women.

Prepare yourself.

Include a start date, a cause for quitting, warning indicators to look out for, and the day on which you will dispose of all cigarettes, lighters, and ashtrays in addition to the date on which you will start your new life without smoking.

You can deal with the things that set off your triggers in different ways, such as by squeezing a stress ball when you're nervous or by drinking tea after dinner rather than lighting up.

You have the option of either chewing gum or going for a stroll whenever a craving comes.

Instead of reaching for cigarettes, go for some celery sticks or tiny carrots that you've prepared as a healthy alternative.

Laundering your clothes, blankets, and towels will get rid of any lingering cigarette smells that could be a trigger for you. It's possible that you'll also need to get the interior of your vehicle detailed.

The Importance Of The Role Of Social Support

Quitting smoking is a major life change that needs to be approached with dedication, resiliency, and support. The availability of a robust social support system is one of the most important aspects in effectively stopping smoking. Throughout the process of quitting smoking, having social support from friends and family may be an invaluable resource for offering encouragement, inspiration, accountability, and understanding. In the following paragraphs, we will discuss the significance of social support and how it might play a role in the achievement of your goal of quitting smoking.

1. Support Emotional Support is an Essential Component of Social Support Emotional support is an essential component of social support. Having people in your life who are empathetic, understanding, and willing to lend a listening ear are essential components of this. The process of quitting smoking can be emotionally taxing, and having people around you who can create a secure environment in which you can communicate your feelings and frustrations can be quite helpful during this time. They are able to provide encouragement when you are going through challenging moments, remind you of the progress you have made, and help increase your self-confidence when you are having doubts. Emotional support can help reduce feelings of stress and anxiety, which can make the

process of quitting smoking much more doable.

2. Encouragement and inspiration
Having the support of friends and family can be a constant source of encouragement and inspiration as you make progress toward quitting smoking. Whether they are members of your family, circle of friends, or members of a support group, people who sincerely believe in your capacity to quit smoking can be an extremely powerful incentive. Their recognition of your efforts, appreciation for your accomplishments, and words of encouragement can provide gasoline for your determination and urge you to keep going in the right direction. Your network of supporters can greatly bolster your self-assurance and determination to kick the habit of smoking by providing you with

encouragement and positive reinforcement.

3. Accountability The concept of accountability is an essential part of the social support system. When you tell other people about your plans to stop smoking, they will be better equipped to keep you accountable for your actions. Your support network may help you stay on track by keeping tabs on your progress, providing you with helpful reminders, and even engaging in some lighthearted competition with you. Accountability partners can give you the extra push you need when things are difficult, which will help you stay dedicated to the goals you've set for yourself. Your sense of duty and your drive to give up smoking can both be boosted by the realization that other people are invested in your achievement.

4. Practical Support This type of support includes providing you with tools and guidance that are more practical and can help you on your quest to stop smoking. It may involve assisting you in making your home a smoke-free zone, providing you with alternative things to do to take your mind off your cravings, or even going to support group meetings or doctor's appointments with you. The removal of potential obstacles and the provision of the tools and resources essential to facilitate the quitting process are both contributed by practical support. Practical support, in any form—whether it comes in the form of a buddy guiding you in discovering healthy coping skills or a loved one assisting you with your daily chores to lessen stress—can dramatically improve your odds of success.

5. Experiences and Knowledge Shared
Making connections with other people who are going through the process of quitting smoking at the same time can be tremendously beneficial. Support groups or online communities offer individuals the chance to share their experiences, discuss different methods of coping with difficult situations, and learn from one another. Participating in activities with other individuals who are familiar with the struggles and achievements associated with quitting smoking can provide a sense of companionship and affirmation. Knowing that you are not the only one going through this issue can provide you with reassurance, new perspectives, and useful tips. When you talk to other people about your struggles to quit smoking and learn from their experiences, you can gain useful guidance and perspective that can help

you navigate the ups and downs of the process.

Begin Making Your Plans Right Away!

Have you given any consideration to starting your own business? You have to get started with these procedures right away in order to guarantee that you are performing the action in the proper manner. This article covers everything from identifying and verifying your idea to figuring out the practicalities of it all and even marketing your brand once it is up and running. It even covers marketing your brand once it is up and running. The following are some of the themes discussed: You won't need to change your approach one bit if you want to be successful in any of the new businesses you have in the works!

You can't just wake up one day and decide that you are going to do something amazing, meet someone important, or see someplace fascinating; you have to make the preparations, even if they aren't obvious. You can't just decide that you are going to do something wonderful, meet someone important, or see someplace intriguing. You can't just decide that you're going to do something amazing, meet an important person, or visit an exciting place. You can't accomplish any of those things. If you want to learn how to speak a different language, for instance, it is pointless to claim that you are going to learn it; instead, you need to start with the basics and build up your knowledge as you go along. Congratulations, you should feel quite proud of yourself if you have already taken the first step toward making your dream a reality.

When there are only three months left until the big day and you are trying to figure out how to begin wedding preparations, wedding planning can be an extremely stressful process. This is especially true when there are only three months remaining until the big day. There are numerous approaches to taking care of the planning of a wedding, none of which are fundamentally superior or inferior to the other possibilities. There are, however, a few strategies that, when implemented, will make your life a great deal simpler and your stress level a great deal more bearable. In this article, we will provide some suggestions on how to get an early start on organizing your wedding so that you won't be unprepared when the big day eventually arrives.

Prepare to start working on your [preparations] straight immediately. This may entail acquiring the required supplies, making the necessary reservations, or even ensuring that you have everything you need to do the task in the shortest amount of time feasible. If you are currently in a city and would like to visit another location, you should make reservations for your travel arrangements as soon as humanly possible. If you want to get a jump start on learning how to speak in Spanish, you should enroll in a Spanish class as soon as possible. Put the plan into action, and begin things moving in the direction you want them to go in, whatever it is you have in mind. When it comes to getting things done, there is no time like the present.

You are free to start making preparations at any moment you see fit; however, you should be aware that it is unlikely that you will be able to finish all that is on your to-do list right away. Be reasonable in your anticipation of how much you will be able to accomplish in advance, and try not to be too hard on yourself if you find that you will not be able to finish everything before the event in question takes place. Instead of getting worked up about things not getting finished on time, direct your energy toward completing these activities as quickly as you can, and use the remaining time of the day to unwind and enjoy your wedding!

Many people find that giving up smoking is a challenging and stressful undertaking they must do. The concept of gradual separation is one way to quitting smoking that has the potential to be useful for some smokers. This strategy calls for gradually cutting back on the amount of cigarettes smoked on a daily basis up until the point where the smoker is able to quit smoking altogether.

The first step in the gradual separation approach is to determine an acceptable daily limit for the amount of cigarettes that will be smoked. If a person smokes an average of 40 cigarettes per day, then on the first day of quitting smoking, the goal would be to cut that number down to 39 cigarettes per day. The following day, the target would be to cut the number down to 38 smokes, and so on and so forth. The smoker is able to progressively acclimate to smoking less and fewer cigarettes as a result of this steady reduction in the amount of cigarettes smoked, which helps reduce the physical and psychological withdrawal symptoms that might occur when stopping smoking abruptly.

When employing the strategy of progressive detachment, it is critical to put in place some kind of support network for yourself. Encouragement, support, and support in the form of helping to hold the smoker accountable for their progress can be provided by a friend or loved one throughout the process of quitting smoking. You may phone the individual every day to congratulate them and encourage them to stay on track with their goals.

It is essential to keep in mind that you should only engage in this method with a person whom you have a deep-seated hatred for and who is willing to engage in this method with you. The process of gradually detaching from something can be a slow one, and it may take several weeks or even months to get to the point where you are ready to quit totally. However, the time and effort required to quit smoking are significantly outweighed by the numerous benefits that can be gained from doing so.

Finding the approach to quitting smoking that is most successful for you is a vital step on what is ultimately a very personal journey. There is some evidence that quitting smoking in stages can be beneficial for smokers, but this method might not be right for everyone. Before attempting to stop smoking, you should have a strategy in place and discuss with your healthcare physician the method that is most likely to be successful for you. It is important to keep in mind that quitting smoking is a process that demands patience and determination, but the rewards for your health and well-being will make the effort more than worthwhile.

Stage Four: Make Arrangements for the Alternate

Your next step is to contact the smoking cessation nurse at the general practitioner's office in your area and make an appointment to visit her. Simply put, this is to ensure that you get the most effective nicotine replacement therapy (NRT). Keep in mind that nicotine addiction is mostly a psychological problem, accounting for 95% of the problem. In spite of this, just 5% makes a difference and might be the deciding factor in whether or not an individual is successful in kicking their smoking habit. While I don't agree with skipping nicotine replacement therapy (NRT), other individuals do. Acquire a sufficient quantity of nicotine microtabs with a dosage of 2 mg. These microtabs, which resemble miniature mints and dissolve when placed on the tongue, should also be accompanied with a 'inhalator' device. A nicotine capsule is inserted into this slender tube made of plastic before being used. This is then inhaled instead of smoking a cigarette in order to receive a "hit" of nicotine through the process of actually inhaling the substance. Inhaling a small amount of nicotine from an inhalator will satisfy that need adequately enough for the body to overcome the craving. Now, the reasoning behind using these types of NRT is that the microtabs provide your body with a baseline level of nicotine, and so they take the edge off very bad nicotine withdrawal symptoms or cravings. On the other hand, the inhalator is used for the times when you really feel the anxiety and tension of desperately needing a cigarette. It is possible that the smoking cessation nurse will suggest other forms of NRT for you, with different dosages depending on the size of your habit. While it is possible that it will be a case of trial and error in order to find the right one for you, I only suggest these specific methods because they have worked perfectly for an addiction of 15 cigarettes per day for more than 20 years. I've also heard that putting nicotine replacement therapy patches on the skin can sometimes cause allergic reactions, and that some people find that the patches make it difficult to fall or stay asleep.

The carbon monoxide levels in your blood stream will be measured by the smoking cessation nurse as one of the helpful actions they will undertake for you. If you get your carbon monoxide levels examined before and after you quit smoking, and observe that after you have been smoke-free for some time, your carbon monoxide levels have dropped to a baseline level – fully free of poison – this might act as a psychological boost and help you feel more motivated to stay smoke-free.

People, in my experience, either end up smoking both e-cigarettes and the real cigarettes alternately, or they end up becoming hooked to e-cigarettes for the long term. E-cigarettes should be avoided at all costs because they serve no purpose other than to replace traditional cigarettes. If you go down this path, you will only be replacing one addiction with another, and the approach that I propose for utilizing NRT is only for short-term use! Just to get you through the worst stages of nicotine withdrawal, which could last anywhere from a week to a month.

Facts Regarding People Who Smoke

These are just a few of the many unfortunate realities that come along with the habit of smoking. Even though smoking has a negative impact on health and wealth, quitting smoking is possible and can lead to significant improvements in both of these areas.

• Smoking is the leading preventable cause of death in the world, accounting for more than 7 million deaths annually.

•The addictive component of nicotine, which is found in cigarette smoke, may very well be on par with that of hard drugs like heroin and cocaine.

•Tobacco use is linked to a wide range of adverse health effects, some of the most common of which include the deterioration of lung tissue, cardiovascular disease, stroke, and respiratory illnesses.

•Despite the known risks to health, almost one billion people around the world still smoke cigarettes.

•Smoking can be expensive, with the average cost of a pack of cigarettes in the United States being approximately $6.28, which can add up to a significant cost over the course of one's lifetime.

•Passed-down cigarette smoke can also be harmful, and exposure to it can increase the risk of cellular breakdown in the lungs and heart disease. •Smoking can discolor teeth and lead to bad breath, and it can also damage skin and hair.

THE IMPACTS THAT CIGARETTE USE HAS ON OUR SETTING

Smoke has the potential to have a negative impact on the biological system by contributing to the contamination of the air, soil, and water, as well as causing damage to the natural life and flora. Smoke from rapidly spreading flames, for example, can send a large amount of particulate matter and toxic chemicals extremely high. This can impact human health as well as the ecosystem by reducing visibility, altering the cycle of nutrients, and increasing the risk of intense fires.

In a similar vein, smoke can have an effect on the populations of plants and animals. The inhalation of smoke can cause problems with a creature's respiratory system, and the lack of habitat and food supplies that can result from intense fires and other sources of smoke can disrupt biological systems and lead to a reduction in the amount of species that exist in a given area.

Smoke has the potential to contribute to environmental change by releasing compounds into the atmosphere that are harmful to the ozone layer as well as other contaminants. This can amplify the effects of a hazardous atmospheric deviation, leading to more frequent and severe severe wildfires, heat waves, and other extreme weather occurrences.

A number of nations around the world have taken steps to reduce smoking, such as taxing tobacco products, enacting no-smoking laws, and conducting public awareness campaigns.

IDEAS TO HELP YOU QUIT SMOKING

You should not give up on quitting smoking even if you have tried to do so in the past but nothing has worked for you. If you continuously trying to give up smoking, you will eventually develop a stronger desire to do so, at which point it will become much simpler to do so. If you want to kick this vile habit once and for all, this step is absolutely necessary. Even smokers are aware of the harmful effects of cigarettes, and the fact that they continue to indulge in the habit despite this knowledge is evidence that they are unable or unable to kick the habit. You will need to educate yourself on how to quit, and you will also require the emotional support of those who are close to you. The following is a list of advice that can assist you in quitting for good.

Believe that you have what it takes to kick the habit. This is one of the most crucial things you can do for yourself. It is possible to have the desire to stop smoking, which is a very significant factor, but if you do not believe that you are capable of doing so, it will be quite challenging for you. You will set yourself up for failure if you believe that you lack the resources necessary to give up the habit. If you want to be successful, you need to put your attention on your mental state because believing in yourself is directly related to how you feel mentally. Consider concentrating on a particularly noteworthy example of anything that you have accomplished in the past. Try to rid your mind of all the negative things you've been thinking by replacing them with more positive ones. Putting an end to one's habit of smoking cigarettes isn't easy, but it is possible, and many people have been successful in doing so.

The inability to occupy your hands with anything other than thinking about smoking is another challenging aspect of giving up the habit. You should give it a shot whenever you get the urge to do anything with your hands because many people feel the need to do something with their hands while driving, which means that you should try to do that whenever you get the urge to do something with your hands. If you are going to be driving, you need to find a technique to prevent yourself from being tempted to smoke by things that remind you of smoking. Consequently, the task at hand is to look for something that you can "fiddle" with, hold in your hand, and transport with you. You might find it to be an odd statement to make, yet there is genuine power in adopting a different pattern of conduct on a daily basis. This will also satisfy your desires, allowing you to resist the temptation to light up a cigarette as a result.

When you are trying to give up smoking, you will need to make certain adjustments to your lifestyle so that you aren't confronted with situations that make you want to light up again. There are several key distinctions and resemblances with regard to that one. For instance, some people find that they enjoy smoking even more when they are drinking alcohol. Any smoker will tell you that their favorite time to smoke is after they have finished eating. Make sure you don't sit in your favorite recliner after meals because that's when you usually puff on your cigarette. You are obligated to make all effort possible, even if it means moving to a different chair after you have finished eating. You have to remove yourself completely from the situations, people, and things that put you in a state of mind that makes you want to light up.

You have been provided with several effective and well-established methods for quitting smoking, which we hope you will find useful. It can be difficult to determine what will work most effectively for you in the long run. If you are serious about kicking your smoking habit once and for all, then you should make an appointment with your primary care physician. Your physician is the best person to advise you on the most effective methods of quitting, including the most effective methods for you in particular.

Let's take a look at some concrete examples of hypnotic suggestions that have assisted other individuals in quitting smoking, as well as how you might apply these techniques in your own life. Hypnotherapist Kevin Hogan, author of "The New Hypnotherapy Handbook" published in 1996, offers a number of recommendations for quitting smoking that have been shown to be successful in clinical trials. The following is a list of some of these recommendations, along with a concise description of why they are effective.

You are going to substitute drinking water for smoking whenever you get the urge to light up. The goal of this recommendation is to get people to switch from their unhealthy habit of smoking to one that is more beneficial to their health, such as drinking water. Consuming water not only helps to satisfy cravings, but it also has many other positive effects on your body and helps you stay hydrated.

You are finding that the smell of cigarette smoke is becoming more offensive to you. This proposal has the potential to make the act of smoking less appealing and, as a result, less desired by linking the smell of cigarette smoke with something unpleasant.

Because you don't smoke, you have a sense of accomplishment and fulfillment. This advice helps establish a self-image as a nonsmoker and supports the positive feelings that are connected with quitting smoking. You can increase the likelihood that you will keep your resolve to abstain from tobacco use if you allow yourself to feel proud of the things you have accomplished.

When you think about smoking, you picture yourself as a smoker, and you quickly come to the conclusion that this is not the kind of person you want to be. This recommendation assists in altering the view that you are a smoker and fosters the idea that quitting smoking is a decision that enables one to become the greatest version of themselves.

Your resolve to give up smoking is only growing stronger with each passing day. The idea that you are able to quit smoking and that your willpower will continue to grow as time goes on is reinforced by this advice. If you have faith in your capacity to kick the habit, you will be in a better position to overcome challenges and difficulties along the way.

It is essential that you make the decision to give these hypnotic suggestions your whole attention and to accept them in an open and receptive manner if you want to get the most out of them. You have the option of either recording these ideas in your own voice or listening to recordings made by a trained hypnotherapist. Spend some time each day relaxing and listening to these suggestions, and give them the opportunity to permeate your unconscious mind and become a component of your experience of the world.

In conclusion, hypnotic suggestions are a potent tool that can assist you in changing your behaviors and freeing yourself from the grip of tobacco addiction. You have a better chance of making changes in your life that are both long-lasting and successful if you select words and ideas that have a strong resonance with your inner needs and ambitions and if you deliver the suggestions in a style that is upbeat and focused on the future.

In the following section, we will go over some of the most important ideas that were covered in this chapter, and we will also give you a sneak peek at what is in store for you in the following chapter, in which we will explain how to use self-hypnosis to take charge of the process of quitting smoking on your own.

In this chapter, we have discussed the power of words as well as the ways in which hypnotic suggestions can change behaviors, specifically the habit of smoking. We have talked about how important it is to choose suggestions that are acceptable and effective, as well as how suggestions can be adjusted and individualized to match the requirements of a given person. In addition, we have evaluated some effective hypnotic suggestions that have been used by professionals in the field and provided real examples of how you might implement these suggestions in your own life.

Throughout the course of this chapter, we have demonstrated that hypnotic suggestions are an effective method for combating addiction to tobacco products. You can gradually change your behaviors and overcome the difficulties that hinder you from quitting by absorbing the recommendations into your subconscious mind and allowing them to have an effect there.

You are now prepared to move on to the next chapter, in which you will learn about self-hypnosis and how to take control of the process of quitting smoking. Now that you understand how hypnotic suggestions work and how they can help you modify your habits, you are ready to move on to the next chapter. You will learn self-hypnosis techniques in Chapter 7 that will enable you to implement hypnotic suggestions on your own, giving you greater independence and control over the process of quitting smoking.

To that end, are you prepared to take charge of your life and educate yourself on the techniques of self-hypnosis so that you can quit smoking for good? Join me in the next chapter, where we'll discuss this fascinating and empowering way to overcoming addiction to tobacco products. You won't want to miss out on this important knowledge, which could make all the difference in your ability to quit smoking successfully.

www.ingramcontent.com/pod-product-compliance
Lightning Source LLC
Chambersburg PA
CBHW050246120526
44590CB00016B/2234